That morning I scrawled
SONG BIRDS
across the blue
and stuck the sticky note
to my wall.
I wanted to remember
what I'd heard.

Apparently, there was a time
people cut out
the tongues of song birds
to eat as delicacies.
SONG BIRDS
I wanted to remember.

That afternoon
my friend Tania
arrived at the backdoor
and screamed:
Come outside!

We ran and *oh my*....

Thousands of little birds
filled the Rosscarrock sky
like nothing we had ever seen
or heard before.
The song birds had returned home
in sound, and flight. Pure as joy.

Everything joined together
as we listened
beyond silence.

Also by Sheri-D Wilson:

Re:Cord CD (2007)
Re:Zoom (2005)
Between Lovers (2002)
the sweet taste of lightning CD (2001)
The Sweet Taste of Lightning (1998)
Girl's Guide to Giving Head (1996)
Swerve (1993)
Bulls Whip & Lambs Wool (1989)

Autopsy of a Turvy World

Sheri-D Wilson

Frontenac House
Calgary, Alberta

Book and cover design: Epix Design
Cover Image: Martin Guderna
Author photo: Heather Elton

Library and Archives Canada Cataloguing in Publication

Wilson, Sheri-D
   Autopsy of a turvy world / Sheri-D Wilson.
Poems.
ISBN 978-1-897181-17-1
   1. Twenty-first century--Poetry. 2. Social ecology--Poetry. 3.
Human
ecology--Poetry. I. Title.
PS8595.I5865A98 2008   C811'.54   C2008-900435-3

We acknowledge the support of the Canada Council for the Arts for our
publishing program. We also acknowledge the support of The Alberta
Foundation for the Arts.

 Canada Council   Conseil des Arts
for the Arts   du Canada

Printed and bound in Canada
Published by Frontenac House Ltd.
1138 Frontenac Avenue S.W.
Calgary, Alberta, T2T 1B6, Canada
Tel: 403-245-2491 Fax: 403-245-2380
editor@frontenachouse.com   www.frontenachouse.com

This book is for
Michael Owen Roberts
my accomplice in life

Acknowledgements

I wish to thank many people in my life for their support, guidance and inspiration.

In particular I would like to thank: Shone Abet, Lillian Allen, Susan Boychuck, Russell Broom, my dear Bell's, David Broderick, Anne Connolly, Heather Elton, Diane di Prima, Ian Ferrier, Kathy Fisher, Judy Gladstone, Michael Green, Martin Guderna, Damon Johnston, Clifton Joseph, Maureen Judge, D. Kimm, Dale Lee Kwong, Colette Macaggart, Shannon Maguire, Annette Mangaard, Hrothgar Matthews, Micki Maunsell, Orunamamu, Laura Parken, Kirk Ramdath, Gabrielle Rose, Sandi Somers, Michèle Stanners, Anne Waldman, Peggy Walden, Edward Washington, Tom Wayman, Maralyn & Bill Wilson.

A special thanks to Allan Boss, Billeh Nickerson, and Caroline Szpak for their poetic guidance and third-eye notes.

I would also like to thank the following for their generous support:
Alberta Foundation for the Arts
Banff Centre (Sarah Iley, Christie Rall)
Spoken Word Program
BravoFACT (Judy Gladstone)
Canada Council for the Arts
Canadian Broadcasting Corporation
CKUA
Heart of a Poet
Kerf Music

Contents

Autopsy of a Turvy World

Autopsy of a Turvy World

I Visited the Bridge of Your Ghost on a Full Moon Morning

Today, I came to visit the bridge of your ghost
like a monument built over mortality
and the weeds and the flowers
grow below the solid line, like capsized dreams.
And I went to the water's edge
where they left you face down
in the mud,
drowned and clubbed to death.

When I was down there
the groundskeeper came by,
to say a mother duck
laid her eggs just inches from where
they left your life behind
for less than a song.
Underneath the wooden bridge—
what the hell went wrong, all graffiti
skulls and half-sprayed words
under there, on the cement wall
pylon beside the place
where they kicked and you crawled—
I sing to you.

I sing to you
a lullaby—sense of senselessness
fills up in hollow blue hue questioning why.
Why you?
Under a noisy wooden bridge
planks and beams shudder and quake,
above my head, rush-hour retreads, snakes
over.

I take digital vigil snaps
of your beautiful imaginary body,
invisible outline wraps
around the tide here still
like a flower, a water flower
where you laid to rest
your final breath, and I can hear you
here, beg for mercy
I can hear you here
clear as spiritual bells
ring in a bowl.
Past midnight, a meteorite,
you write prayers across the sky.

I want you to know, I sing to you
in praise, and I hope you might hear me
as the night heard you cry,
through the wooden bridge
above, like a racket, rattle dust overhead.
Was it heaven you thought you heard
above you, like a calling
overhead, circling like vulture-angels' tell-tale
tattle, and the herring in the water still
and the heron's priested shore,
and the gates open above the bridge
to the other side
where you might live again?
Gates where you might live again
in your teenaged body like a long note
of stolen youth and eyes of naked wonder,
body unlocked to love
and all the births you might've had.
The streets grow quiet
and the ducks brood on their eggs

and all that remains of life
is death and memory and ghosts and my song
humming
still humming along—

Today, I came to visit the bridge of your ghost
where people cross everyday
on their way in and out of their lives
en route over bones, sticks and stones
cockle shells, easy ivy over.
The sacrifice of a flower
and a heron and a weed and a clam
and a blackberry bush, and a final hour.
Crow calls to me
and I try to understand
without meaning.

Reason is a name on a gravestone
I once saw. Light breaks
and when does hatred rest—
and the wash of excitement and the rush of relief
and the disbelief
that they actually killed you
with sticks and stones,
and they did break your teenaged bones
and their names will always hurt me.

Barre None

In that brief suspension
between upright
and hitting the pillow
sleep—

her mind slides
to her crib,
first prison

memory:
look out from
behind lockdown bars
inside crib trap

mobile
overhead—floats
cardboard ballerinas
twirl pirouettes
blow, dance, blow
one trick prima

look down
braces on legs
immobile

infant custody
un-strap leg bars
bird trap
danse zoo
no tutu

perform
prison break
pas de deux
with obsolete cradle

climb up
over bars of crib,

bourrée along window sill
wide enough for twinkle toes
reach three-quarter point
extend foot down,
développé under hem
of red baby curtains

reach toes, touch down
surface of mother goose table

foot of freedom
échappé

onto table
then off the red
mother goose chair
pas de chat
to centre floor

into red slipper-shoes
red housecoat
out bedroom door
front door, *grand jeté*

first
run away
at five

awake
slow walk
with moon

red as satin
ribbons
sirens silent,
fresh snow breaks
fall

feathers

porté

Autopsy of a Turvy World

Black Diamond
Baby's her name, dig it?

she gyrated in her terra firma gown
through the sex game
around and around
the block so many times
she doesn't even see the signs,
she's a hotrod dragster burn-out

she's the Styrofoam cup
that got tossed too many times
on the landfill
she rides the apocalypse
like a pony, beast with seven heads
and ten horns

tango xango mango
she shakes her tambourine

she's had every hard knock knock
from asphyxiation to gangrene,
she played the scene,
radio active rhizomes
became her toiletry-terrine
atomizer filled with poison mist,
her bottle is filled with tears

just before fall, full moon sky,
shadows stretch like age marks
call the ground, crawl like an animal sound
as it moans, just before it dies for winter
this big city girl, dressed in wilderness hair
dances a lost disco, ergo beware,

doesn't trick like she used to
trick, no liquidation lick,
she's come unchained

she opens her legs for every chair
still drunk most of the time
to forget the johns
she dressed up for,
and the sidewalk blues, and the crack
she laid down for
beside meters
out-of-time

she hallucinates
tries to forget the knife she held
above his head.
the only one
she ever loved,
as he dreamed of someone else,
how he woke up
and left her there,
so she turns on the oven,
and down with the lights
drinks from her bottle filled with tears

she's twinkling like little votives
strung along beads of days gone by,
five-foot-two, eyes that do
the aftermath
destitute, prostitute
and her breasts push up in her tattered bra
till there's nothing left
of the wire, for hire and hire and hire,
and she's left her factories far behind
like so many lovers left cash on her dresser
without even saying good-bye,
she sucks in the gas

she might be old but when she strips
she's got the seven wonders
of the world under there,
when she speaks
she's a country tune—filthy and full of hurt
she's the carriage before the hearse
the morning after the night before
and we love her, Guadalupe curse,
and she's the death star wish
in the sky of her soul,
she's the messy drunk in the kitchen
out of control, she's a path of broken dishes
on her way to a rescue mission, emission,
sensitive as a reef
choral singing deep song grief

we want to visit her
but we don't want to live there,
oilslicked beach red tide poison
she remembers when he kissed her wrong
so long ago she's forgotten,
her father's shyster song
she takes another swig
head close to the stove

in her land mind
she stands at the centre
in the middle of the sky
and she screams for an echo
and the big dipper Y is her landmark
upside-down,
she dances another sex-grift song
she can't even fathom
what the hell went wrong

Black Diamond Baby's Kali,
she's a Zion icon,
she's tired and weary, she's
ruby-lipped Madonna-tipped,
mercy she's the Mother Mary,
more than a CO_2 theory—
in her land mind she digs
for lost belt buckles
the head of the bull
lost horns and buffalo bones
but she's blasted and she collapses
against the fence post in her mind
twigging for true nature
mascara running down
before she blacks out, pissed to the gills,
and the extra pulp in pulp biofiction
is always stranger than pills

her mind flips back
black out Black Diamond Baby
and her aftershock
echoes through the oven racks

when they met
she told him their relationship
had an expiry date,
she gave him all the signs infrared
but he didn't listen,
'cause he was counting his chicken
before he got laid
and he looked into her eyes
like it was the first time he ever breathed
green gas with a perfume disguise, right there
beside the red and pink shiny sink
in a bathroom full of transparent
pomegranate seeds

into the moon she wore an early face
and then they waltzed from ruin to ruin
toward dawn, and then he felt up his dream girl
she moaned her Black Diamond drone,
once more, uncrossed her legs,
her apron's apocalyptic pocket poem, came
unstrung before they left the kitchen
and moved their feeding frenzy to the bedroom
and there they went from bed to bong
from bed to bong, all night long
like a hookah snake stoned on smoky smut
he couldn't get enough of her—
loveless, land use or abuse

they danced and sang
and spun around
in a love twister flame
too fast to see past
insane or profound, supernatural
insane, tectonic ticker
beat a fault line toward cardiac arrest
and the earth cracks,
beast with two backs
tsunami, they erupt with waves
and then
in solar flare despair
she doesn't know what she's doing there,
wildfire blaze, ultra violet rays
and the lava spills like a gash might bleed
toward ever-after disaster
cyclone speed riding bareback,
meteorite impact,

Hurricane Medea,

chair hanging in a tree
and bones and feathers and chills of rattle
the morning morning-after

whose fault lines?

no alarm clocks
he thought
I've never been fucked like that before
and then she showed him the door

Get out, she slurs,
I don't know who you are
you're just another person who did
the earth, dig?

Toronto Taxi Cab

Why do we automatically
trust cab drivers?

She was attacked
three times in her life,
two were by
cab drivers.

The day was slightly overcast
as she left High Park in a rush
looked down at her watch,
the walk out of the park
took longer than she expected
she was out
of time. *Damn!*
Late again
I can't be late again.

Boom

she sees a cab
stopped at the red light
right there, in front of her
waiting at the intersection—
a beacon,
a way out of her time jam
Oh hail thee mighty cabbie. She makes
a run for it. Split-second squeeze,
boom, in the back of the cab,
Queen Mother Café—Queen Street West, if you please.

Cabs are unintentional
travelling time capsules.
They're moving
worlds inside the city. One-way
time machines into the future, for hire,
they inspire motion.
Stranger at the wheel

from a parallel universe maybe,
something unreal
who always knows
which way to go, and the right thing
to say when you're sad or lost
in need of spiritual advice—
Queen Street West; pause, no answer, weird.

Wait a second,
Don't you think we should be turning off?
Black billfold on the backseat floor,
open, not hers, like it was thrown there,
credit cards spilling out, also weird.

Excuse me
Which way are you going?
Curly snake of the car radio coil
hangs over the driver-side visor,
talking piece
swinging back-and-forth,
like a pendulum
catches the eye.
as the cab driver starts a breathless laugh.

Danger. Danger. Cab one forty-seven.
Memorize cab one forty-seven, one forty-seven.

Turn off at the next light.
The cabbie doesn't turn,
just continues to laugh.
Light just ahead
turns yellow. Don't make the
yellow, don't make the
yellow light. Red, red, red.

Adjust body into
jump position. Someone's knapsack
spills out on the passenger seat.
Laughing, laughing
he won't stop that laugh.

Get ready to
jump. Don't
miss this light.
He's going to
keep the cab rolling,
slow enough
now, get ready,
steady

Jump!

          Roll!

                 Toward the meridian.

Traffic flies by
on her side
that side, many lanes
lines, lines, solid lines. Blurs of colour,
slow-motion sounds,
horns, like trumpets, blare.

Cab driver chases.

Run!
Through traffic
freeway, lane-by-lane,
solid line-by-line, like a wild animal.

Tight squeeze, like a
miracle and an accident
at the same time.
Heart pumps through skull,
over fence, climb over fence
jump into new unknowns
down side street, and

free.

Shrink-wrapped in panic, walk
of terror, in each breath
a step of fear,
and goose bumps of horror
all at the same time. With each step
through the tree shadows,
she puzzles the story together.
He must've mugged the real
cabdriver in the park,
moments before she jumped
into the backseat of the cab.

She took him by surprise,
he hadn't calculated
on a passenger.

She stops, thinks of the real
cabbie, and calls
the cab company:
It was cab one forty-seven,
cab one forty-seven,

one forty-seven!

An Amazing Rabbit

You know,
I met this old guy
down in Taos.

Amazing guy,
named
Peter Rabbit.

I got to talking
with the rabbit.
Amazing guy,
started
the first commune
down there
in the United States of America
in the early Sixties,
friends with Timothy Leary,
the whole bit.

Anyway,
I asked Peter Rabbit
what his trick was,
how he stayed
so young,
so long.

I mean this guy was
close to 80,
and he didn't seem
a day
over 60.

And Peter Rabbit
turns to me

in all his glory
and he says:
I just do a little acid
every day.
Just a little acid
every day.

Girl who was Born in a Bubble

She was born deep
inside a pocket, of air,
an air pocket—
surrounded by a thin skin of water
like a single drop, or a thought.

And she looked out
from inside her bubble
like she was looking
through the lucid film of dream, into
another realm, perhaps
she thought, I have a 1000 year cycle,
but she didn't, or maybe she did
in bubble time.

Girl who was born in a bubble
never felt like she belonged,
like she was an outsider—
so she called herself special,
suspended.
And she'd tell people she could stop time
with her bubble magnetism,
she'd say: *Watches explode on my wrists.*

She tried to keep track of her life
find out who she was,
so at night she'd remove
the tiny lock from her diary,
which held her peace-of-mind together
and she'd look inside
like she was watching someone else's
bubble life, from the outside.
And then she'd try to make sense,
draw conclusions, line-by-line

and from time-to-time, she'd freak out
lock it up, and then she'd
hide her diary someplace safe
from herself, somewhere she might
never find it again; and again.

Once, she was stung by a wasp
isoperimetrics rushed her to emergency,
red light, ambulance, amber alert.
Lucky, hospital was her second name
so the nurses knew how to prick her
with needles, without making her pop.
When she recovered from the wasp reaction
she realized her visions improved,
and everything went bubble smooth
after that, in bubble girl world.

She took up extreme floating,
bought a brand new double-bubble wand
performed imaginary circles beyond
her wildest dreams, the new acoustics
inside her bubble
made her opalescent
and her sphere altered in colour
with every mood-ring swing
she was like a living bubble jet,
and she dreamed of doing impossible things
like joining the roller derby.

No regrets. She was fascinating to watch
from the outside, like a zoo animal,
bubble cage, bars. And she'd
watch herself too,
in the bubble skin mirror
convex reflection, full body, 24-7.
The only thing she couldn't see
was a way out
of the bubble.

Until one night,
one crazy night—
in that twilight hour,
when the dying come back to life
for a second—
she started to shrink
she became, thinner and thinner
and she developed
those little black dots
on top of her orb,
that all bubbles
worry about, and then,
bubble girl's bubble popped!

It just popped—
different than a snap—
it popped with a popping sound, popcorn
pop, champagne
bubble pop, bubble wrap pop
pop, bubble gum pop
like culture or pop music; pop, pop.

She broke her bubble
right there in the middle of
an unsuspecting puddle,
with other raindrops
popping all around her
on the oil-slicked pavement
in the middle of the Wal-Mart parking lot
while other's shopped, she just
popped into, or out of
this world. Her lights went on,
like a little bubble big bang
in one easy pop,
she just popped, like a weasel, or whatever

goes pop, she blew her top
and her bubble,
like a thought,
disappeared.

Once you pop you can't stop the onslaught
of pop, there's no going back.
And you start to notice other possible pops,
you didn't see before,
like pregnant women or heroin addicts.

I hope they name me after a season,
she thought.
She looked at a picture that was taken
when she still lived in the bubble
and realized, it was the only proof
she had been there
at all.

Hobby horse with training wheels,
nothing makes any sense,
like trying to saddle
a seahorse, teeter-totter,
freedom squatter
ring the bell jar,
her sanity brings her flowers,
because she is in the world
but not of it.

Broken Mirror Year

Twelve months of isolation devastation,
lonely, only worse,
like she couldn't get invited to save herself.
Hot pepper up the nose, an adverse curse
the opposite of messiah
she felt like an outcast unwanted pariah
place where nuclear waste goes and then grows
and then goes and glows and grows a-glow,
like she was invisible.
No one could hear her cry.

She lived in a one-room box with four walls
and a door, and there was a foamy on the floor
in the corner like an empty raft, afloat
with a ring-less alarm clock
like a misplaced suicide note, on which to dream.

Time told
with no ring.

She shared the bathroom with a clown
who got drunk and cried a lot.
Sometimes he'd sleep around
to make himself feel worse,
and sometimes she'd wake up to his
late-night weeping, and imagine
his stretched smile, make-up running down
his blue heart and his red nose.

Next day they'd go to work
at Kaleidoscope,
and they'd make masks
of gargoyles, together.

One time at 4:00 AM,
bored stiff, she went to Beacon Hill Park
and clear-cut an entire tulip bed,
wore gloves to avoid getting
caught—finger/petal flower/prints.

In August, that same year
she dropped a mirror which broke
in two pieces, and a bathroom stranger said:
You'll have seven years of bad luck,
like some kind of tragic punch-line to
an already ill-fated joke.

So the next day she went to the Sally Ann
and bought twenty-five looking
glasses: two-way, magnifier, vanity,
rear view, make-up, full length,
and a telescopic optic for hand-held fears.
It all adds up to one-hundred-and-seventy-five
star-crossed years of sheer
catastrophe, black cat-astrophe.
She thought,
is it possible to carry your omen points
into your next life with you?

She carried her mirrors
back to her single-room filled with make-shift
vases of dead tulips, and she smashed
them, one-by-one—
as a test—
twenty-five mirrors,
and one-hundred-and-seventy-five years
of bad luck, to dispel.

She laid the broken shards
out on her floor, like a carpet of misfortune,
and looked down at herself
in the debris, looking up at the ceiling
queasy feeling, and she was reeling,
as she told herself, don't take another step,
every eye ever opened has looked inside
this kind of vertigo once. She asked herself,
How will I ever know if I have
good luck or bad
after this?

What are the rules of superstition?
Does the break have to be a mistake?
And who
gives a reflection permission?

As a test,
she glued the traumatized mirrors
onto large panes of transparent glass,
to piece the clues together in plain view,
and the clown, who helped her stick them there,
said:

They look like a sci-fi forest but they'll never last
the glue will let go one day
and the world will just fall away,
slide into shattered chaos. Oh yeah.

But to her, all at once the mirrors looked like
splinters of trees, an eclipsing world,
fragments of sky
and stars and time to reflect
and she started to play with her candlelight flame
and the mirrors came to life, sent out animal cries,

the way light and dark intersect
refract, like a dance of fire on four walls,
she thought.

And she moved
the mirrors like she was their sea
all luminous strand
inside her lonely room like a forgotten secret
she looked into the other side
and saw what she had never seen before
first hand—
as a test—
and it was then
that she used the illusion
to make herself
disappear.

The next day,
the clown called
the Superstition Society
to report her vanishing—mysterious
as full moon Friday the 13ᵗʰ—and after he called, a black
cat crossed his path
when he walkd under the ladder, by accident,
rabbit foot held tightly in hand
to dispel his reflection, on her resurrection
—to undo what she had done
with the mirrors,
he thought—
he put bread in his pocket
threw salt over his shoulder
turned around three times
knocked on wood
buried chicken bones under the rhubarb in the garden
spat at the evil eye,

and went to bed
with a spoon under his pillow.

Didn't sleep a wink,
but in the morning
he opened his skeleton umbrella,
the one he used for clowning, without cloth,
to redo what he had already undone
—to undo what she had overdone,
he thought—
and then it snowed
right there in the house
and he knew, right then
he would never see her again.

Underwater Cages

He went down
as he always went down
in a cage.

It was his underwater dream
come true, to go down
in a cage.

Down he went
to visit the great whites.
It was his underwater dream.

And their teeth
and their hunger
through his bars.

He wanted to tempt them
and yet it was they
who were free.

I wish I'd known sooner
there are no endings—
no conclusions to be drawn,

only
extensions of a line
that look like waves,

and the dream
of going down
in a cage.

Fall Showers in Spring

Just as she thought,
He's been in the shower
for a very long time,

she heard the splish-splash
whoosh-crash, squeak of flesh,
against porcelain.

She sprang up, ran tripping,
spoke through the bathroom door,
Are you all right in there?

Inside, *I think so.*
Out, *Should I come in?*

In, *Come in.*
So she opened the door

and there he was
lying on the floor,

of the shower
with his dick still in his hands.

He said, *I guess I passed out*
from the heat.

Next time you masturbate
in my shower, she said,
lie down first.

She turned to leave
and that's when she noticed,

crocuses peeking
through the cracks

in the floor.

Ma and Tight Corners: Tipsy Curvy

"It goes like stink!" ~ Ma, 1969

It was a turquoise
1957 Chevy
with the truck engine.

And Ma would drive that old jalopy
around corners, hell bent
like a Formula One demon on speed,
and she'd yell, *Hang on!*
We'd be in the back seat
changing from our school clothes
into our brownie uniforms,
and she'd take the corner
with a fighting spirit, on two wheels,
and we'd hang onto the seats
for dear life, gripping with our fingertips
till our lips turned psych ward white,
and then both car doors on one side
would go flying open,
no holy shit handles
we'd hang on to that front seat
with the fake fur seat covers
so we didn't go flying out…
Whoaoooo…
…and then the corner would be over
and the heavy '57 Chevy doors
would come flying shut.

Bang!
        Bang!

And we'd go back to changing our clothes
and eating our Kentucky Fried Chicken
right out of the barrel, like pros,

finger lickin' good, back then, before seat belts
and car seats and sun block and water wings.

Back then, when they'd give us
matches to play with
and guns to shoot the bottles
lined up on the fence
for fun.

Back when you could ride without a helmet,
feel the wind in your hair.

Back then.
It was a turquoise
1957 Chevy
with the truck engine.

Because of Ma
I've never been afraid
of the dark. She taught
me how to stay on my toes,
dance with danger.
And she's funny. Damn,
she's funny. Always
makes me laugh.

Sometimes
it scares me
when I think
I might be
like her, on two wheels.

Hang on!

Moon remembers Cuba as she

pushes her body against the sky
she looks down,
and describes a large veranda
high up from the street
where her people
gather
to celebrate the birth
of a very old woman
in the middle of Havana
on a full Moon night

Moon remembers Cuba
as she
describes the smoke
of Shaman's cigar
as it rolls like a voice, from below the sea
new messages from old revolutionaries,
and when he laughs, it breaks in waves

Moon remembers Cuba
as she
describes herself—
making a slow pass
behind the distant lighthouse
Moon beam
beacon halo, optic illusionary—
into the perfect spot,
eclipse of light
until her people
high up from the street
on the large veranda
can not distinguish
whose light is whose, or
which light is which

they all stop mid-revelry
they fall under her spell
charm of lighthouse light
house lighthouse
Moon
she looks back at them
eye of a temptress,
solstice festoon
full of high jinx and hallelujah
pupil gold as alchemist soul
to guide, and warn

and the two pictures
lighthouse and Moon
slide into one another
as lovers navigate truth,
they slide into one other
hold the picture
embrace, in Tantric breath,
slide into one another
body-into-body of light
as a lifetime, in suspense

moments pass
and no one in all of Cuba moves,
deep inhale in-breath-in
dance, groove of
stillness, in drum,
heat trance of
not knowing, beyond drum,
beat of
silence, in sound, speech of
flowing, air bound, levitation
not knowing
words, just vibration,

love says everything
in surrender, a kind of death
so beautiful, the door remains
open, to the other side
pharology

and Moon sees this
and she smiles

she describes how finally
the very old woman breaks
the silence
with a sigh, *La Luna,*
and the sound breaks
liquid
and everyone goes back
to living once more

Connecting the Dot

for Diane di Prima

She said:
Choose a dot, any dot in front of you. Now look at the dot. Stare
into the dot. See nothing but the dot. Just sit there and look at
the dot until you know the dot well.

Now, choose another dot. Just choose any other spot, another
dot, and stare into the new dot. See nothing but the new dot,
until you know the new dot like you knew the old dot, well.

Now, choose another new dot and stare into it. Get to know it,
like you knew the other dots. Stare at it as long as you would like,
until you know it well.

Now, let your eyes go back to the other dots you already know.
Let your eyes switch dots quickly.

She said:
Sometimes all you have to do is change your gaze. You think
about one thing, and you change to a new thought. Change your
gaze. Look at a new dot. Find a new dot to look at. Sometimes,
it's the only way you can survive.

Experiment with Monolithic Thought

Part One: Vivisection of Einstein's Brain

Ten percent—they say,
I only use ten percent
of my brain,
right, left, right, left, right
as two minds
overlap, con-
fused

If my brain could do my feeling,
would my heart begin to think?

And what percentage
of my brain do I use,
for imagination, perception, observation
intuition, meditation, reflection
divination, shun, shun
and dream—what about memory,
telepathy, fantasy, déjà vu
healing—oh what a feeling
does that count?—and prayer—
what about eternal despair?

If my heart could do my thinking,
would my brain begin to feel?

Ten percent—they now say
is a myth-illogical neuro-mistake,
simple screw up
Einstein might have made,
then again
twenty years after Einstein's death
didn't they discover

Einstein's brilliant brain was stolen
from his dead-head body, yeah,
later didn't they uncover
the rough pearl of genius
preserved in a mason jar?

It's true, the autopsy physician
who opened Einstein's head
stole his brains as a souvenir
of non-common-sensical quizzical
"thinking"

Deduction: Brain Abduction

And in studying Einstein's brain
didn't they conclude
that his genius was due to
parts of his brain
that were missing all along,
and that's why Einstein's thoughts
made the jumps they made,
cause there was nothing in the way
to stop them, no thought blocks;
or maybe Einstein's brain
over-compensated somehow, into—
a cryonic suspension
the mind-bends, synapses snap
in time with possibility,
and the annus mirabilis
mastermind sees light in spectrums,
synaesthesia, with emotion
alternative illumination,
and colour-fields open to
time travel, traversing the mind
as he did

And what are the thoughts
that connect the dots
of humankind?
Maybe if we were all missing
ten percent of our brains
we'd be geniuses too.
Albert Einstein-ified

Of two minds

Part Two: Test Tube Humanity
The Guinea Pig Poem

I hear you were a test tube baby
now you're a movie star.

I hear you got plastic surgery
and died, to look ten years younger
than you are.

Strange how
we're all human guinea pigs
research lab rats on the go,
human test subjects
round-and-around
Jane Doe, Jane Doe, Jane Doe.

Who decides *let's blast the A-bomb?*
Whose decision is it to stay home?
What are the results of a nuclear test,
I hear the new ring tone is a rotary phone.
What's in the past, is not past.

I hear in World War Two
they invented the death ray;
military invention unsurpassed,
now it's a microwave oven,
to time save, oh to save time, that's fast
Flash Gordon fast!

And what do we die for, and how do we live?
Is germ warfare a bio-weapon or a crime?
Both!

Who will answer
the soldiers in Iraq
when they come back
uranium-ized by their own bullets?
Will they be traumatized
when the U.S. government, anaesthetized,
won't pay for the contamination test—
a thousand bucks too much.

And the soldiers will die of cancer
with a medal on their grave
grave hearts—
when there was no one
to save
in the first place; where do we start,
stop, start, stop, start—they call them nuclear
guinea pigs.

If my brain could do my thinking
would my heart begin to feel?

For the guinea pigs
who get paid cold cash
to receive injections
of contagious infections?
When does waste become trash?
And side-effects, more than a back lash
of the multi-national corporation eyelash,
one blink, snap, you're dead.

Bye-bye.

And while the low-paid "volunteers"
put their life on the line
for a piece of the pie,
politicians and scientists
keep promising to keep promises
take this, take that,
it won't kill you, you won't die.

And the rest of us
laboratory rats, we do it for free,
as they push product-after-product
on us, we greedily agree—
in fact, we pay them for it,
birth control pills that kill
and sadistic lipstick
as women die of cancer, another statistic,
and no one wants to talk
cause it would cost
the pharmaceuticals too much in stock—
botox, lines of communication, gone.
To the moon Alice, you're a pawn.

Ten percent—who's only using
ten percent of their brains now
over-compensating somehow, in vain,
for a lack of vision.

The incision—
life is life, when it's life
and the last breath, death, right?
There is no conclusion
just optical illusion
delusion,
and canning for the winter.

You Need to Get Your Head Examined

The nice young man
in the clean white coat
tells us not to wander
around the psych ward alone, he says,
These are the bughouse rules.
Bugaboo hullabaloo,
ho-ho-hee-hee-ha-ha.

We're here to dance
the Tarantella, the Czardas, and the Polka
for Ponoka's so-called crazy folk—
we take the attendant's advice
stay close to the theatre,
so as not to provoke or entice
further madness.

You have to know,
this is back in berserker days
back before jails became mental
institutions, back before asylums drugged
their patients to ignore
the core reason they came unstrung
in the first place,
almost back to bedlam days
when they still used shock treatments
straitjackets, and frontal lobotomy
I plead insanity. Let me out of here;
set me free, I want to climb
the monkey tree, ho-ho-hee-hee-ha-ha.

The *theatre* where we'll dance
for the lost minds, looks like an oversized
puppet-play proscenium set
for an enormous Marionette,
with a basketball net on one end
and a make-shift stage on the other.

The windows are sky high
and they all have bars
like prison, a downtown
apartment or a cage. He tells us
to dance without aggression,
to tambourine death
without rage.

I want to climb an invisible ladder
rung-by-rung, find a hidden
sage unsung; for humanity, I want to stop
the insanity, release the lock, throw
away the escapee key.

In Ponoka,
I feel a certain madness climb
like it's living in the walls
wisteria vine up my spine,
like it's rising from the floor,
as church walls absorb prayers,
I can hear the bughouse door
lock shut and the musical chairs,
and the circular stairs
to the bath of ice cold waters.
I feel the chill you feel
when the ghost of a madman
who never found rest, walks through
the asylum, and into
the marrow of your bones.

Backstage, in the wings,
entirely
alone.
The other dancers have left
to find food
I thought I'd be safe
inside. *Sshh! Quiet!*

I execute a half-baked
warm-up, slightly spooked,
and then decide to give in
to distraction
and snoop—
something to silence my unsound mind.

For instance,
what's in that pile in the corner
of the backstage floor?

I rifle through
the clothes, piles of clothes,
think: Loony-Bin Rose,
and who knows who these clothes
belonged to, Nellie Bly
before her faux-crow-pose

I suppose,
or some other lunacy legacy,
lived inside this skirt or tormented shirt.

Exhibit One:
A faded red sweater, missing
pearl button, feels like cashmere—
imagine it worn
by a woman,
near perfection
who was sterilized, for her moon's
hot desire; think of Tantric pleasure
and how do you measure
the kind of madness that would drive
a wanton woman higher and higher,
'til some straight and narrow relative,
becomes scared, and has her committed
to electric
shock waves.

Dig through the crap,
what's this? Some kind of—
off-white straps.
I stop, in my tracks.

It's a straitjacket
right here, backstage
and it's worn to the thread,
use restraint, I think,
don't scream.
You can't let this out
of your head
tread, the distorted dream
that you're living, instead.

There's no one here—just steal it,
stick the straitjacket in your ballet bag
and take it home.
No one will ever know, but you.

Do they still use these?
They do, do they?
They do.

No, you can't steal from the theatre
it's against the sub-culture credo
gypsies never steal from gypsies.

But it isn't a real theatre.

It doesn't matter.
If you take this straitjacket,
you will never sleep
again, it's a bad omen.
Think.

So what. Take it.

Don't.

Take it.

Don't. You'll have to live
with the souls who were strapped in.

No. That's crazy-thinking.
Take the straitjacket.

Don't. Do. Don't. Do.
Don't, don't, don't. And I didn't.

If it was now
I'd take it, as evidence.

And I think,
some people feel guilt
for what they do,
other's feel guilt
for what they don't.

Lost Love Found

Once upon a grave
her grandmother gave her
a small bottle
with a single golden drop inside,
her grandmother said:
save this one drop of perfume
to wear behind your ear
when you fall in love
she thought,
amber drop,
an entire forest, distilled.

And she kept that sweet opium bottle
with a single drop of perfume
inside,
for years and years, she
carried the drop of golden perfume
locked fragrance of longing
from room-to-room, from country-to-country
she packed and unpacked
but she never undid the lid.

Always wondered
what that one perfect drop
might smell like
behind her ear,
if she dared fall in love and open
the golden lid, apple nectar
inside,
and the response of her lover
would resonate beyond the grave

until one day she lost
the bottle

                it slipped away
with the magic potion, inside.

        It was in
        a breakup with someone
she could not love,
        and her bottle with one drop
        fell into the hands
        of an unknown stranger.

Dreams evaporated
        like passion.

        Now, in a state of love
she reflects on the drop,
        and she knows someone has opened
        her bottle of Eros
'cause she can feel the scent
        from *here*.

        The tincture has released
its long attachment
        to ideals.

Ode to the Raven Omen

A few months back
I was at the Banff Centre,
Rocky Mountain high,
to attend a techno-conference
with a small gang of super-geeks.

Anyway, it was spring, and I was sitting,
and the boogle of über-techno super-geeks
were sitting outside having lunch
on this beautiful sex-licked day—
printemps, all Stravinsky and jasmine—
when I hear this:
whu-whu-whu-whu-whu
coming up behind me.

I knew it was the sound of wings
but these sounded like really large wings
like Tyrannosaurus Rex wings,
coming up behind me:
whu-whu-whu-whu-whu
and then *Doof,* on my shoulder.
I look over and it's a Raven,
a real live Raven just landed
on my shoulder like I was a tree,
or something.
Crazy.

Anyway:
pinnnnnnngggggggg

someone pushes
the remote control pause button
and in one wild moment it's like
everyone and everything turns to stone
geek greek-freeze, stunned-stone.

I look around and everyone's frozen
in time, blue screen, with cafeteria lunch
trays en route to their tables, mid-word,
mid-step, like a lost civilization
embalmed mid-air. Half-eaten
sandwiches en route to their mouths
some mid-bite, others
mid-swallow. And the
Raven's acting like
everything's normal
sitting there on my shoulder,
looking around.
So I whisper to the bird:
Whatever you do right now,
don't shit.
Don't shit right now, that's all I ask.
Everyone's looking
and if you take a crap right now
it will ruin everything.

The bird seems to understand
gives me a little Raven nod
and then goes about normal
Raven business,
takes another bite
of my sandwich and:
whu-whu-whu-whu-whu
flies off into the mountain's
easy distance.

And I'm left
sitting there, with the frozen
gob-smacked geeks, and then:
pinnnnnnggggggg

someone hits the remote un-pause pause
and stone clicks into life,
all the clocks kick-in
start ticking again
statues start moving,
released from Medusa's rock-face myth
stunned
we're all sitting there
changed somehow in a glance.

And then
after a long pause
one of the geeks
pipes up and says:
Oh my God,
I think we just had a Harry Potter moment!

Trance,
whu-whu-whu-whu-whu
hhhaaaaaaa

A Slippery Slope: Anti-Aging & the Skiing-Peeing Story, all in one

The other day
I meet this young whippersnapper, who says:
So, what was it like in the olden days, before mini disk-players!
Yeah. Mini disk-players, the olden days,
my mind reel-to-reels, performs analogue covered wagons.

So I told this young whippersnapper iPod,
how I skied before the invention of snow boards,
which he couldn't conceive, *B.S.*, he says.
Before Snowboards, I reply,
back in the days when there was still snow, to blow.

We were the real ski hot dogs, even
before they invented hot dog stands in the Big Apple,
we were the Professional No-Style Team
six chicks, extreme-theme.
And I told him we'd take our old cassette players
the ones that looked like a small shoe box
or a Black Magic Chocolate Box,
and we'd duct tape them onto our bodies
like suicide bombers before our time,
iPod, way back before Walkmans
we figured out how to scc God.
Yes, we'd strap on our headphones,
smoke a fatty,
press GO Led Zeppelin GO
Pink Floyd GO Hendrix… only *classiques*
for the freaks, wired for sound.
We'd ski
down the mountain's
high strung tunes,
we were Raven mountain
monsoons, ballistic-chicks.
Not re-mastered like some re-erected
slick dick that's never felt the inside
of a pussy without a second skin.

Oh no, I told him how we'd blast
through those mega-bumps
like Mach 5 G-force hyper-sonic
Super Nova Tank Girls
on 220 Rocket Skis
Dark Side of the Moon on our head phones,
K2-Solomon-Head's beneath our lace up boots.
We'd hit the moguls, hard core, max air
speed bump, extraordinaire
shooting stars, to the cosmos, sunshine,
we were the real meal deal,
even before McDonalds ruined real.

We were nasty-ass good-old bad-girls
even before there was a word for Avalanche,
we were skiing off the sides of mountains
like sticks of pistol dynamite, aerial snow angels.
We took double Black Diamond runs
like they were bunny hills,
even before you were even imagined
by your Mommy and Daddy,
we were reverberating to the ice-crystal
chorus of an unnamed Snow Goddess
called *Nature-rama*!

The whippersnapper says:
>   *Oh now you're*
>   *dating yourself.*
And I say:
>   *No, actually I'm*
>   *dating someone*
>   *younger than you.*

Oh yeah. We even had chairs. There was this one day in early
spring, so spring
even the snow thought it was hot.
And the Professional No-Style team
was standing in the long lift-line
stoned out of our minds, wineskin
through Ray Ban moonshine, in the sunshine,
when we heard this high-pitched scream
this blue murder bellow,
coming from the patch trees, just above us.
Everyone in the long lift-line turns around to look,
What's going on in the trees, up there?
It's still too early in the season, can't be a bear.

And well, I guess she was a beginner.
And I guess she went in the trees
to pee. And I guess,
she pulled her one-piece ski suit
down around her knees. And I guess
her skis started to go down
the slope. And I guess
she didn't know how to stop
because she was a ski bunny.

And she came blasting out of the trees
at warp speed, and geeze-Lake-Louise
she was screaming, but she's not thinking
cause all that screaming
attracted everyone to look.
And Lady Godiva divine
flew by the long spring ski-lift line
with her one-piece ski suit down
around her knees,
flailing behind her now
like an inflatable lovecraft, a blow-up unitard,
screaming and peeing and skiing
all at the same time.
Multi-tasking she was

past the howling ski-lift line
with a long hilarious yellow trail of misfortune
almost Olympiad pee extending behind her
like a golden tail of bad memory—

Later, in the lodge,
I told her she could get an endorsement
for that kind of embarrassment.

And then,
it hit me, whippersnapper,
we're all going down hill,
but it's really about how,
it's about how
we go down.

Borderline Neuroses:
Psychosis between YYC and LGA

Down a double 007 martini,
in the airport bar.

Why do they call it air travel
when there isn't any air? And "airport security"
must be some kind of *nom de guerre*. Air
tight.

Oxygen deprivation, X-ray calibration,
terrorist isolation, taser termination.
Travellers, eyes glazed over
like deep-fried do-nuts,
feel caught in some extraordinary act
of desperation.

Post-911 security gate
crackdown in dire straits, run by
a snarling Cat-in-the-Hat cynic
armed fully automatic, symptomatic
of a system on the skids, panic attacks
run rampant, real as the risk
of a stampede at Mecca, and paranoia.
Never name a teddy bear Muhammad,
if you know what's good for ya!

Love those long line-ups
they give you time to zone out
contemplate osmosis
halitosis, of the person
too close behind.

Security Inspectors:
Thing One, Thing Two
Three, Four, and Five.
Zombies alive, in ultra-stiff
stuffed into blue
gained-a-few-pounds uniforms.
Diligently irritated
on the edge of a new
no-name bad mood,
no one can understand,
as the Things go about searching
for something that isn't there.
We despise them collectively
but act cool
like nothing's happening,
cause we don't want to get caught
doing nothing
like them.

They X-ray my purse
as it glides by like a privacy hearse
picture in reverse.

Oh my good God
that guy at the end of the security,
Thing Five—the laptop swabber
looks exactly like Shakespeare Larry.
I met Shakespeare Larry
when I was a teenager.
He was a model and an actor.
I think that's Shakespeare Larry.
Act natural
like nothing's happening.

Larry was always older
and everyone flirted
with him, cause he was dignified
and once Larry told me
in his English accent
that I was beautiful,
and I couldn't believe it
knew it wasn't true,
but I liked the way he lied—

Walk through.
Walk through.

Beep, beep, beep, beep, beep
airport security sound
reboot, execute, smile,
smile, not too happy
just an ordinary smile, maybe
an innocent non-significant
unsuspecting smile.
Smile, nevertheless calmly
act nonchalant.

Sidebar:
There's something you should know
I'm travelling to the U.S. of A.
with a bandolier of bullets
in my suitcase
down below.
Already checked in.
But I don't know if they know.
It isn't the guns that kill us, it's the bullets.
Do they know?

Electro-magnetic smudge, I wonder
how he got to do, what he does.
Maybe it's my bra causing the
disturbance.
If they nab me now
will they get me for smuggling,
or will it be trafficking?
I don't intend to sell
the bandolier of Rambo-esque bullets
in my bag.
Maybe I should've thought
this one out more.

I could say, *the bullets are a fashion
accessory*. A performance prop.
I didn't know they were real.
Did I say that out loud? My heart's
beating through my head
out my temples, it feels surreal.
Damn, how did I get this far
into the prank, without thinking?
It was a party joke, for Gods sake.

That really looks like Shakespeare Larry.

My nose hair clippers?
I've got enough ammo
in my bag to perform
the entire shootout
at the OK corral, and you
want my—

"Nose hair clippers."

Aren't they called snippers?

"Whatever, I have to confiscate—"
she grabs them.

Bastard.
Don't you find it weird,
how I can carry a bullwhip on board,
but I can't carry
nose hair clippers?
She shoots me a click-click-ballistic
glare, and I shut up.

Note to self:
Don't crack jokes
at security.

Fine, I say, *but just one minute,*
And I hand her my Starbucks coffee
and bag of Starbucks cookies,
and then I grab my nose hair clippers back,
I'm going to be away for ten days, I say,
I better do this now,
snip, snip, snip, clip, clip, clip, clip, clip.

There you go. They're all yours now.
I hand them back to her,
uniform issued 50 pounds ago, now
having trouble breathing —
she looks horrified,
rubber gloves and all, but she
takes my nose hair clippers back,
like a dirty diaper
between her pointer and thumb—
and puts them in that special place,
where all nose hair clippers go.

She hands me back
my Starbucks coffee and pot cookies,
which I conveniently slip-switched
into the Starbucks cookie bag
just before the security gate,
and I'm on my way—

bandolier of bullets
safely checked in,
and my pot cookies securely in hand.

One last thing
Larry?
"My name is Harry."
Larry.
"Harry."
He sneers through his teeth,
"My name is Harry."
Right, Harry, I must've mistaken you
for someone else,
like Larry.

I walk away
knowing it's him, Shakespeare Larry
with an English accent,
and I wonder who's security now,
and why would anyone change their name
by one letter.

Are we running up or running down?
As I ride the escalator along the ground
walk toward my gate,
airlessness of a flight
held tightly in mind, like a boarding pass.

I take one last look back
at Larry, or Harry,
or whatever, Thing Five,
and he's trying to look
innocent
through his teeth
in the distinct shape,
of a smile.

Funny thing, a smile.

Phoebe and the Key Factory

Phoebe
thinks
of
skeletons
when   Mary
says: *just*
throw   away
your   keys
to   life
while   you
still   have
time,
before
they
turn
in
on
themselves
s
s
s
.

Phoebe has no idea
what her sister means,
and continues to collect
keys; obsolete keys, keys
to everything—to nothing, keys
that no longer open anything,

keys to wrecking-ball houses
and junkyard cars
drawers of keys;
in her mind.

Mary knows Phoebe loves
skeletons, and she thinks
of their parents. Phoebe
became estranged
many years before.

Counterfeit Diet

"There is no darkness but ignorance."
~ **William Shakespeare**

Part One: The Feast of Foodlessness

All this food, and nothing to eat
as we fill, filler-up, refill our, fill
our feeding-frenzy faces
with more sweet treats, and enough
gross sucrose, to redefine refined,
count our days as if it were time
light another cigarette
simulate a stimulant, and forget,
it's Russian roulette.
Hurry up
   and lie down.

Enrich yourself. Oh fortify
before the nutrition mortician
comes to mortify,
to deliver another body bag.
Ziploc the freshness in,
let the autopsy begin:
perished by heart
attack, high cholesterol snack
after snack—bury the cadaver
secret sauce slather,
beast feast, now deceased
expired neck deep in trans-fat grease.
Lie with the lard
   wiped out, sucked up by junkyard food.

And the Prize in the Cracker Jack box—
a fresh slice of seedless watermelon
and a strawberry the size of a grapefruit,
steroid fruit-aphonic, mutation turned to chronic
as a million little replica raspberries
that all look the same—like mutant clones—

scream at us from their containers.
Rows and rows of clone-berries,
in little clear coffins
like plastic boxes with labelled crosses,
lined-up at the grocery store graveyard.
Every little berry the same size,
colour, and shape—
they don't grow
in the garden like that, and they know it.
Clone-bone berries, freaking out
homicidal, out-of-control, screaming—
as they're forced to conform to the same size
to match each other, like Pringles—no singles
shingles. It's like our fruit and vegetables
are screaming with roid rage,
ster-roid rage, like genetically engineered
wrestler-fruit, colossal but unpredictable
food that fits container conformist bits
no pits, or seeds but grow humungous
at speeds even a murderer finds scary.

And speaking of scary: what's with those
friggin' little baby carrots? Oh my God,
they are the freaks of the carrot world,
I had a bag of those baby carrots
in my crisper for six months
and you know after six months
there wasn't an iota of rot
on the little orange buggers.
Can't kill them no matter what you do
they simply will not die,
like breast implants, impenetrable,
imperishable and yet still edible,
back lash
                    snack lash!

All this food, and nothing to eat, Twinkie.
The only way to sell an apple
is to cut it into slices, we
want everything done for us, up the prices,
like our bodies are convenience stores
replacement receptacles for love.

Billions and billions served
          eating themselves to death.

Fast-
          Food
Death-
                    by
Drive-
                         thru
Drive-
                              by

Death-
                                   thru
Food-
                                        bye

Death
          Breath

Part Two: Lenny's Leftovers

One fry at a time—he died
one fry at a time.

Lenny my ex-landlord *lived* on
mayo-slathered double obese burgers,
deep-fried chunks of Chubby Chicken,
chocolate-chip shakes,
and gooey simu-cheese Tacos.

Poor Lenny,
addicted to snack-er-tainment,
caught every cold bug going—
he was a growing-factory
for super-sized mucous. Disease.

Every morning when I left the building
I'd take twenty Vitamin C's and ten cold FX's
just to walk past his door.

But what perplexes,
is that Lenny didn't die
of his grocery cart
Lenny died of a broken heart.

I wish I'd taken
the time to speak with him;
he didn't even bother to leave a note
because I suppose he knew
no one
would come
to find it.

I realized I couldn't identify
him, the man
at the morgue, because
I only knew him by
the names on the bags
of takeout food.

Part Three: Bummed Out Three Times

The raspberries must be bummed
they all look exactly the same,
like the breasts of all the women in L.A.—
       and hey
       have you heard
       you can't even cremate
       those fake tits, turns out
       those boobs will not break down
       no matter what you do to them
       in the crematorium—
       those knock-off knockers
       have to be removed
       and returned to the loved ones,
       along with the urn of ashes
       I suspect—objects of desire.
       Don't worry,
       when they are returned to you,
       you can recycle those silicone bunnies
       reuse them, like retreads, maybe
       sell them on e-bay one day,
       at a reduced rate of enhanced proportion
       a measurement of compromised distortion
       eyes bigger than their artifice
       22 carrot gold.

Also bummed must be
the 24 people who perished in 2003
with a rare lung disease—
       contracted when they inhaled
       the butter flavour vapour released
       from a fully-popped bag
       of microwave
       popcorn.

Survival of the lucky, death by popping.

Also bummed—
        were Mike and me
        in a restaurant recently
        eating over-priced miniature food,
         wondering if we should save our seeds.

Part Four: Ambrosia Noir

Aroma, mouth-watering night
Ambrosia noir, soma
every bite, taste of
mid-summer night heat
epicurean masterpiece
in darkness, beside fire
circle of fire, we eat—
in darkness of night,
by moon light
we taste, senses anew
holy food takes on,
life of its own, holy chow.
Where was this food grown?

Deep in Tao?
How might one piece of mango
wild in salmon taste?
In foreign tongue
ten thousand taste buds
in one gastronomical moan
place-to-place, into unknown taste,
in the darkness of night, by fire light
olfactory opera ignite—
ka-boom; zow-ka-pow
in the dark, swimming upstream
to river womb
like a tropical spawn on the tip
and all along the top
of a dance-filled sustenance
mango tango on the tongue
artichoke heart in the dark
explodes with sensation beyond creation
lands me in perfect view
the ocean point of you

fierce as delicious sea
in the darkness
I make you out in flavour.

Holy *sacra manna!* Between us
you are all the places I've ever seen,
or not, been to,
all the lovers I ever loved
people I ever met
books I ever read, the times I crawled
and flew. You are all things I carry with me
the times I bled, stones of starvation
bones of inspiration, rattle moon,
in a dark room, I still perceive your light
thru the taste of you this night
at a distance almost taboo,
cave of savour every morsel
like a song, of you
a funeral of light birth
belong with you
taste of night so aware
it awakens me, each bite
to all time. And a kind of silence
only darkness can hear,
near senses of gold—
captured animal, a rare herb
chase of wild, five-year-old
child unleashed, superb,
kind of freedom
fulfillment every bite.
Ambrosia holistic
taste of night, darkness
reminds me to stop
at sweet, sweet, strawberry

stop, at cream, oh cream
is that coconut? stop
strawberry, cream
alone, with silence
and you, living dream,
taste of the first time
like touching the tongue of God
with a poem,
intrigue of raspberry heart.
Ambrosia, I will start
at the end. Where has this
silence been?
All I hear is pure joy.

living between Ontario & Quebec

*The Cezanne apples have a unique importance to me
that nothing can replace.*

~ Gertrude Stein

in a cheap grey concrete island suite
on Broadway, so to speak, in Vancouver—
out front down below, off-and-on beat,
rush-hour bumper-to-bumper
heat wave hi-way street,
and I'm sucking up the fumes,
emissions, exhaust

give me silence
long silence
no telephones
no alarm clocks
or door bell buzzers
no mail in-and-out

living between Ontario & Quebec
in a grey block in the middle
of the block, funeral home
mortuary out back, through the slats
in the blinds, the order of the golden rule
in purple neon, reminds of rewind
and I'm sucking up the fumes
emissions, exhaust

give me silence
at any cost, no lawn mowers
or back-up beepers in reverse
no car alarms, or the cursed mufflers
broken, no racing motorcycles
late at night, or
ambulances, sirens, static stop

living between Ontario & Quebec
a different time than now,
before cathedrals converted into condos
and squares turned their prayers
to a bull market stock,
tick talk, back,
not before electric shock
and the atomic clock, click clock,
but back when people bought car alarms
from the store below, and the demo—
be-de de-de de-de de-de
ba-da da-da da-da da-da da-da da-da da-da da-da
do-dah do-dah do-dah do-dah
ee-dee dee-dee ee-dee dee-dee

all day long, asylum song,
stop the noise

            pull a U-ey
            back from whence, same song different tune
            blink back, way back, before crack
            hit lotus land streets, before delete

living between Ontario & Quebec
and traffic and a funeral home,
and that damn
funeral home's leaking obscene green
embalming fluid. it's just running
out and down the entombment's
exit-way, green zone
into the alley
behind my rat-trap cheapo pad,

with the brilliant view of
the Expo ball, on Broadway
it flows down,
like a green inner-city
death stream
into the gutter,
the metropolis manhole
out my back door,
funeral home driveway
spews green mortician-ooze
down the lane, down the drain
like an oil spill; ocean suffuse
it flows down,
a day-glow akimbo, akin to limbo
absinthe dream, a nightmare,
death row
mummifying the alley,
like a death-green
nuclear waste machine,
taste of ill-fated
futures yet to come,
as we preserve our faces
to delay decay
place our dead on display,
the undertaker wears a respirator
and our waste just wastes away,
I hear pet taxidermy's
the hot new thing
so you can freeze-dry
Fee-fee forever, stuff her in the corner
frozen wag
the green slips inside
makes us look alive,
for a last glimpse
after we up, we up and die

and it spins down the sewer
in a grateful dead dervish
as I do the dishes
look out my kitchen window
with the bullet proof glass, and watch
the toxic fluid
as spirits drift and pass—

and pass, and drift and pass and
pass, as the spirits drift and pass
and pass and pass and pass

is this the time for love songs?
is this the time to put flowers in the barrels
of their guns?
does the poet protest by not speaking love,
until the haters stop pushing hate?
while all humanity is going down the drain
just put me into the refrigerator
embalm me later—

   My obit reads:
   when a butterfly is born
   there is a single drop of blood
   released

   still life of moving fruits
   optical illusion of motion
   all Cézanne
   like a still death
   you want to touch

Fortis et Liber

Oh, I love you Alberta
Big sky beautiful you, strong woman,
ruff and soft soft blue
I'm sitting right in the middle of miles of you
High on my ponderosa pony
Saddle smooth and sexy beneath me
I want to ride the range of your possibility
I'm Alberta bound baby; hear the silence of your immensity
I want to touch the horizon of your immeasurable light
Ride the westerly wind of your raven flight
Pow
Pow Wow
Let's go

Golden trail. Light sinks, just west of highway 22
As me and mini gallop wild-west to the crest of you
Ah! Your light stops us in our horseshoe tracks in awe
Even your shadows fall gold – alchemist maw
In the background your a capella sky that impossible colour
It would seem, beyond,
beneath me ponderosa pony ponders – amber dream
Find a feather
Find a feather

There's something ancient about you,
buried deep in your badland bones
Hoodoo voodoo queen,
your heavenly body sings aurora high notes –
flood lights,
I ignite—this night—firefly rare
I am tongue tied, moonified,
I am sanctified, satisfied as a studified mare
By your light – Oh Alberta, your light turns me on –
Bar Bonbon
My big horse Mini is of course,
all a' whinny, all a shimmy beneath me, over you
Oh yeah,
I want to drink from your milky-way river

I want to bucking-bronc scream from your highest peak
Mount Columbia 13,000 feet
Hey lucky stars up there…thanks for birthing me here…
Certified Albertafied – Grade A Canadian girl

I fell for you as a kid
Stubbed my toes on your gopher holes
Shucked the pearl from your prairie oyster, witnessed first-time
eyes of newborn foals, picked whole bouquets of full rushes for
my mother, played hide-n-seek between jails and hails and bales
of hay like none other, like every other, tumbling tumbleweed
Looked into the forbidden eyes of grizzly, bare
Alberta bound baby,
stars fall in the mischief of your eyes as we drop off
Like late season flies,
or crab-apples wind plucked from their branches
And when we rise, in the morning,
ad manum from more
You Chinook arch above the foothill floor,
merge and diverge, animal to the core
Through dawn's early dew,
we roll against the earth moving earth
Like a couple of crazy coyotes,
howling with instinct
Half wrangling, half untangling –
sliding across the slippery Prairie grass
Cacophonous, as one,
in the path of your bright morn-light stream
Cream all buttermilk,
pussy willows and crocuses as we stream-steam
Black gold. Light crude.
You've got gas—it's nasty
It's natural.
It's rude
It's our earth
Our drinking water.

Saddle up ponderosa pony
Pow
Pow Wow
Let's go
I turn –
And Ono, I smell winter in the air
Let's get home before she snaps her snare
Gotta put the plastic on the windows
Suddenly it's freezing, my skin is peeling off my face
My only prayer is thermal underwear
Get me out of this hideous place
Alberta, you're a brutal hard uncompromising crone
And I hate you and I want to leave you,
     live somewhere else that's warm, I moan
And just when I'm ready to throw in the bone,
     I smell my first lilac of spring breath –
     buzzing bees swarm bring honeycomb
And that's when I know, these Buffalo plains,
     they're home
Big sky beautiful you
Strong woman in the ruff, oh yeah, of blue
Wild rose tough; you're my heartland shaman guru
You're God's country, for God's sake
Pow
Pow Wow
You're a Goddess country, for Goddess's sake
Goddess

Poet, performer, film-maker, educator, producer and activist, Sheri-D Wilson has six collections of poetry; her most recent, *Re:Zoom* (2005, Frontenac House), won the *2006 Stephan G. Stephansson Award for Poetry*, and was shortlisted for the ReLit award. She has two Spoken Word CDs (arranged by Russell Broom), and four award-winning VideoPoems: *Airplane Paula* (2001), *Spinsters Hanging in Trees* (2002), *Surf Rave Girrly Girrl* (2004), and *The Panty Portal* (2008), all produced for BravoFACT. Her other Awards Include: Global TV's Woman of Vision Award (2006), SpoCan Award (2005), Bumbershoot Heavyweight Title for Poetry USA (2003), Gold Award at the Houston Film Festival (2003), Three ACE awards (2003), AMPIA (2003, for best short or vignette), CBC Face-off (2002)

Of the beat tradition, in 1989 Sheri-D studied at Naropa University's Jack Kerouac School of Disembodied Poetics, in Boulder, Colorado. Since founding the Calgary International Spoken Word Festival in 2003, Sheri-D has worked at quantum velocities to present one of the most respected Spoken Word Festivals in Canada. Driven by the passion to connect people, voices and ideas she founded/organized SWAN (Spoken Word Arts Network, 2007, 2005) and is the Program Director of the 2008 Spoken Word Program at Banff Centre.

www.sheridwilson.com
www.calgaryspokenwordfestival.com

ORIGINALITY OF ORALITY